Borderline personality disorder

An information guide
for families

D0932811

Centre for Addiction and Mental Health
Centre de toxicomanie et de santé mentale

Library and Archives Canada Cataloguing in Publication

**Borderline personality disorder: an information guide
for families**
ISBN: 978-0-88868-819-4 (PRINT)
ISBN: 978-0-88868-817-0 (PDF)
ISBN: 978-0-88868-818-7 (HTML)

PM083

This publication may be available in other formats.
For information about alternate formats or other
CAMH publications, or to place an order, please contact
Sales and Distribution:
Toll-free: 1 800 661-111
Toronto: 416 595-6095
E-mail: publications@camh.net

Online store: http://store.camh.net

Website: www.camh.net

This booklet was produced by the following:
Development: Caroline Hebblethwaite, CAMH
Editorial: Jacquelyn Waller-Vintar, CAMH; Pauline Anderson
Graphic design: Nancy Leung, CAMH
Print production: Christine Harris, CAMH

3946 / 03-2009 / PM083

CONTENTS

ACKNOWLEDGMENTS

This information guide came together because of the interest and hard work of a team of dedicated, knowledgeable people. It was the leadership and commitment of Sharon LaBonte-Jaques that moved this project forward. We would like to thank Virginia Carver for agreeing to work with the team, to research and to write the first draft of this guide. The following project team members helped shape the content and the earlier drafts: Karyn Baker, Christine Bois, Allison Potts, Barbara Steep, Sonia Veg, Janice Weston, Gwenne Woodward and Monique Bouvier.

The following people provided expert contributions within their fields: Jennifer Foster, Barrister and Solicitor, Health Law and Policy; Wende Woode, BA, BSP, BCPP, Drug Information and Drug Use Evaluation Pharmacist.

A special thanks goes out to the following professionals and family members who reviewed early versions or sections of this booklet and provided invaluable insight and feedback. The reviewers include: Anonymous (submitted without a name), A Family Member, Dr. Deborah Azounsy, Dr. Bob Cardish, Dr. Eilenna Denisoff, Kathryn Haworth, Tammy McKinnon, Jothi Ramesh, Diane and Guy Richards, Barbara Steep, Dr. Charlene Taylor, and Dr. Johnny Yap.

The following people were involved in making changes to the guide using the feedback and recommendations provided throughout the process: Sharon LaBonte-Jaques, Monique Bouvier and Sylvie Guenther.

We also thank Caroline Hebblethwaite for her guidance and advice as our publishing developer. Further, the CAMH Creative Services team of Krystyna Ross, publisher, Jacquelyn Waller-Vintar, editor, Nancy Leung, graphic designer, and Christine Harris, print production co-ordinator, helped make this project a reality.

The content of this information guide was developed using many sources for reference and we acknowledge the work of the following experts in the field of borderline personality disorder: Cynthia Berkowitz, Martin Bohus, Robert J. Cardish, C.J. DeLuca, Frances R. Frankenburg, Robert O. Friedel, John G. Gunderson, J. Hennen, G.S Khera, Klaus Lieb, Marsha M. Linehan, A.J. Mahari, Caroline P. O'Grady, Joel Paris, Valerie Porr, Christian Schmahl, W.J. Wayne Skinner and Mary C. Zanarini.

PREFACE

This booklet is for those who have someone in their lives with a borderline personality disorder (BPD). We hope it will encourage you and your affected family member or friend to seek the information and support you need to understand borderline personality disorder and to begin the journey of recovery.

Because the booklet is written for individuals and families in many different circumstances and communities, it may not address everyone's needs or questions. You will see family referred to many times. When we say family, we mean both family and friends. You can use your own definition and include whomever you want as family and friends.

The first two sections provide information about BPD, including how it feels to have BPD, the stigma associated with BPD, the prevalence of BPD, its symptoms, diagnosis, causes and other disorders that co-occur with BPD. The third section provides information about treatment of BPD, the fourth section describes how to support someone with BPD and the fifth section discusses self-care strategies for partners and family members of those with BPD. The sixth section talks about the importance of hope in the recovery process.

At the end of this booklet on p. 43, you will find a list of helpful resources including contact information for finding treatment, and print and web-based resources. You will also find a glossary and a family crisis information sheet for you to use.

1. About personality disorders

Borderline personality disorder is the most common personality disorder among the several different types of personality disorders listed in the text revision of the *Diagnostic and Statistical Manual of Mental Disorders (DSM-IV-TR)*. This manual is used by physicians and registered psychologists when they make a mental health diagnosis.

The *DSM-IV-TR* defines a personality disorder as "an enduring pattern of inner experience and behaviour that deviates markedly from the expectations of the individual's culture, is pervasive and inflexible, has an onset in adolescence or early adulthood, is stable over time and leads to clinically significant distress or impairment." Someone with a personality disorder generally has difficulty in dealing with relationships and social situations, handling emotions and thoughts, understanding how or why his or her behaviour is causing problems, and finds it hard to change to suit different situations.

2. About borderline personality disorder

What is BPD?

> The best way I have heard borderline personality disorder described is having been born without an emotional skin, no barrier to ward off real or perceived emotional assaults. What might have been a trivial slight to others was for me an emotional catastrophe, and what would be a headache in emotional terms for someone else was a brain tumor for me. This reaction was spontaneous and not something I chose. In the same way, the rage that is often one of the hallmarks of borderline personality disorder, and that seems way out of proportion to what is going on, is not just a "temper tantrum" or a "demand for attention." For me, it was a reaction to being overwhelmed by present pain that reminded me of the past. (Williams, 1998)

Borderline personality disorder (BPD) is a serious, long-lasting and complex mental health problem. Though it has received less attention than other serious mental health problems, such as bipolar disorder or schizophrenia, the number of people diagnosed with BPD is similar or higher than these disorders. People living with BPD have difficulty regulating or handling their emotions or controlling their impulses. They are highly sensitive to what is going on around them and can react with intense emotions to small changes in their environment. People with BPD have been described as living with constant emotional pain and the symptoms of BPD are a result of their efforts to cope with this pain. This difficulty with handling emotion is the core of BPD.

Some common symptoms displayed by a person with BPD include:
- intense but short-lived bouts of anger, depression or anxiety
- emptiness associated with loneliness and neediness
- paranoid thoughts and dissociative states in which the mind or psyche "shuts off" painful thoughts or feelings
- self-image that can change depending on whom the person is with; this can make it difficult for the affected person to pursue his or her own long-term goals
- impulsive and harmful behaviours such as substance abuse, overeating, gambling or high-risk sexual behaviours
- non-suicidal self-injury such as cutting, burning with a cigarette or overdose that can bring relief from intense emotional pain (onset usually in early adolescence); up to 75 per cent of people with BPD self-injure one or more times
- suicide (about 10 per cent of people with BPD take their own lives)
- intense fear of being alone or of being abandoned, agitation with even brief separation from family, friends or therapist (because of difficulty to feel emotionally connected to someone who is not there)
- impulsive and emotionally volatile behaviours that may lead to the very abandonment and alienation that the person fears
- volatile and stormy interpersonal relationships with attitudes to others that can shift from idealization to anger and dislike (a result of black and white thinking that perceives people as all good or all bad).

The types and severity of BPD symptoms experienced may differ from person to person because people have different predispositions and life histories, and symptoms can fluctuate over time.

The term borderline personality disorder was coined in 1938 by Adolph Stern, a psychoanalyst who viewed the symptoms of BPD as being on the borderline between psychosis and neurosis. However, some experts now feel the term does not accurately describe BPD symptoms and should be changed. Some also feel that the existing name can reinforce the stigma already attached to BPD.

The road to specialized treatment and recovery is often hard because the symptoms of BPD can make the affected person emotionally demanding and difficult to engage and retain in treatment. As a result, the disorder is often stigmatized and helping services may be reluctant to accept clients with a BPD diagnosis.

However, with appropriate treatment, people with BPD can make significant life changes, though not all symptoms of BPD will disappear. Remission is more common as people reach the middle years of life. Hope and recovery are important to both the person and family members. These issues are discussed in more detail on p. 39. "The overarching message of 'recovery' is that hope and meaningful life are possible. Hope is recognized as one of the most important determinants of recovery" (O'Grady & Skinner, 2007).

What feelings are associated with BPD?

I feel empty and lonely, sometimes like I don't exist at all, and saying my name feels like a lie because I know there's nothing inside. I play roles, try to be who I'm "supposed" to be, and I'm good at being anyone but me. I fill in the space with what's appropriate—my goals, careers, values, it's all based on the situation. I want to feel something, anything other than nothing. I go from okay to suicidal in an instant and don't even know why. But one constant is a sense of worthlessness that spills over into a desperate need for self-destruction.

— a client

Borderline personality disorder can have degrees of severity and intensity, but at its most severe and intense the emotional vulnerability of a person with BPD has been described as akin to a burn victim without skin. The tiniest change in a person's environment, such as a car horn, a perceived look, a light touch from another person, can set a person with BPD on fire emotionally. Some of the extreme feelings associated with BPD have been identified and include intense grief, terror, panic, abandonment, betrayal, agony, fury or humiliation.

Family members have feelings around BPD as well. They have described living with a person affected by BPD as constantly "walking on egg shells," never knowing what will trigger an outpouring of emotion or anger (DBTSF, 2006).

Family members may often feel manipulated by their loved one, but any perceived manipulation is not deliberate. The person living with BPD is trying to manage and deal with intense emotions that greatly affect his or her behaviour.

How common is BPD?

Studies in personality disorders are at an early stage of development. Community surveys of adults have indicated that the prevalence of BPD is close to one adult in 100, similar to that of schizophrenia (Paris, 2005). The most recent (and largest) community survey in the United States found a prevalence of BPD of six per cent. At this time, we don't have accurate rates for Canada (Grant et al., 2008).

It is unclear whether BPD is more common among women than men and some reports state that about 70 to 80 per cent diagnosed are women. Other research suggests that although there are more women in a treatment setting, there is no significant difference between the incidence of BPD in women and men (Grant et al., 2008).

How is BPD diagnosed?

In Ontario, a physician, a psychiatrist or a registered psychologist can make a formal diagnosis of BPD or any other mental health disorder. The first step toward diagnosis is often with a family physican or the emergency department of a hospital. If there is enough reason to be concerned about someone's mental health, the family physician can make a referral for further assessment.

Whoever makes the diagnosis will use the *DSM-IV-TR* to ensure that the person fits the criteria for a diagnosis for BPD.

What other disorders co-occur with BPD?

It is very common for someone with borderline personality disorder to have other mental health problems that can complicate the diagnosis of BPD. Some disorders that commonly co-occur with BPD include major or moderate to mild depression, substance use disorders, eating disorders, problem gambling, posttraumatic stress disorder (PTSD), social phobia and bipolar (manic-depressive) disorder. Sometimes it can be difficult to diagnose BPD because the symptoms of the co-occurring disorder mimic or hide the symptoms of BPD. As well, relapse in one disorder may trigger a relapse in the other disorder.

When does BPD begin?

Like the onset of other serious mental health problems such as schizophrenia, the symptoms of BPD appear in late adolescence or early adulthood. In some cases, parents may have no warning that something is wrong; their child who had appeared to be functioning well suddenly falls apart with the onset of behaviours such as emotional outbursts and suicidal gestures.

What causes BPD?

As with other mental health disorders, our current understanding of BPD is that a person's genetic inheritance, biology and environmental experiences all contribute to the development of BPD. That is, a person is born with certain personality or temperamental characteristics because of the way their brain is "wired," and these characteristics are further shaped by their environmental experiences as they grow up and possibly by their cultural experiences.

Researchers have found differences in certain areas of the brain that might explain impulsive behaviour, emotional instability and the way people perceive events. As well, twin and family history studies have shown a genetic influence, with higher rates of BPD and/or other related mental health disorders among close family members. Environmental factors that may contribute to the development of BPD in vulnerable individuals include separation, neglect, abuse or other traumatic childhood events. However, families that provide a nurturing and caring environment may still have children who develop BPD, while children who experience appalling childhoods do not develop BPD.

Though histories of physical and sexual abuse are reported to be high among those with BPD, many other experiences can play a role for a child who is already emotionally vulnerable.

Stigma and BPD

In the world outside I met ignorance, stigma and judgment.
I felt isolated, stressed, full of guilt, shame and fear.

— *a client*

Many societies look down on people with mental health and/or substance use disorders. They and their families face negative attitudes, behaviours and comments. This is known as stigma.

Stigma can:
- shame, isolate and punish the person who needs help
- reduce the chances that a person will get appropriate help
- reduce social support
- lead to lower self-confidence
- make the person feel that he or she will never be accepted in society.

Family members also experience the effects of stigma. Their social support network may shrink and they may face negative attitudes if they reveal their situation. We know that the risk factors of separation, neglect or abuse in childhood have been associated with the development of BPD in some people. Because of this, family members may be blamed and may feel or be seen by others as "part of the problem."

Newcomers to Canada may experience greater stigma because of their culture and what is considered acceptable within that culture. Sometimes even asking for help can be difficult for someone whose culture does not encourage counselling or outside help. They may have difficulty finding the service they need because the counselling is not available or when it is, it is not in their language.

Some therapists are reluctant to treat people with BPD because they are seen as being resistant to treatment and because of their emotionally demanding behaviour. Their tumultuous relationships, mood swings and suicidal gestures can provoke anger and frustration in the therapist. Some programs have formal or informal policies that refuse treatment to people with BPD. Advocacy groups have also identified lack of funding for research on BPD, and exclusion of BPD from research studies.

Sadly, people living with BPD often experience more stigma than people living with other mental health disorders. More information about understanding stigma, experiencing stigma, surviving stigma and combating stigma can be found in *A Family Guide to Concurrent Disorders* listed under Publications on p. 44 at the end of this booklet.

Stigma and BPD with a concurrent disorder

It is common for someone with borderline personality disorder to also have a substance use or other addiction problem, and the stigma experienced by someone with one disorder is magnified for those living with two or even more disorders. Negative and blaming attitudes toward those with substance use and mental health problems (concurrent disorders) are often internalized, and a person with concurrent disorders may experience social isolation, poverty, depression, reluctance to seek treatment and loss of hope for recovery, as well as prejudice and discrimination when seeking health care, housing, employment or other services. Again, *A Family Guide to Concurrent Disorders*, listed on p. 44, is an excellent source for information on stigma.

3. Treatment for people with BPD

Treatment didn't make my BPD behaviours go away completely like I thought they would, but I noticed that I could measure the time between episodes of self-harm in terms of years and I continued to use the coping skills I learned.

— a client

What types of mental health services are available?

In the past, specialized treatment for BPD was hard to find, but the disorder is now being better recognized and diagnosed and more communities have established specialized treatment programs that significantly improve outcomes for people with BPD. However, the complexity and variety of BPD symptoms and their overlap with other psychiatric disorders continues to make accurate diagnosis difficult and time-consuming. For those affected and their families, there may be frustration before the right mix of help and resources can be found.

Services for people with mental health problems include hospital emergency departments, acute-stay hospital beds, extended residential care, as well as outpatient care provided by hospital outpatient services, community mental health clinics, assertive community treatment (ACT) programs or private practice psychiatrists, psychologists and other health professionals. There are also services that provide a variety of programs including housing and employment support, drop-in services and peer support. Some people may prefer to receive services from a health or social service agency, doctor or health practitioner providing language or culture-specific services. More information about specialized mental health services in your community can be found by contacting Mental Health Service Information Ontario or your local branch of the Canadian Mental Health Association. Further information on these and other resources is listed on p. 43. Health professionals such as your family physician, a nurse practitioner or social worker may be your first point of contact. They can determine whether they can assist you and your affected family member or whether you may need a referral to more specialized services. In smaller urban or rural communities, family physicians may provide the majority of mental health services and are often the primary support for people diagnosed with BPD.

Treatment for serious mental health problems such as BPD will usually involve:

- education about BPD (psycho-education) with discussions on what is known about BPD and its causes, what kinds of treatments are available, how to self-manage BPD and how to prevent relapse
- psychotherapy or counselling on an individual or group basis
- prescribed medication for specific symptoms of BPD such as mood swings or anxiety.

In most cases, treatment will be on a community or outpatient basis, but some people may require a period of stabilization in hospital if they are experiencing severe symptoms such as suicide attempts, self-harming or psychotic behaviours. Being in the hospital can also give doctors the opportunity to review a person's current medication regime, start new medications and monitor their impact.

Specialized and effective treatment for BPD requires a long-term commitment, often over a number of years. Families can benefit significantly by obtaining support to better understand BPD and developing their own self-care strategies.

What happens when BPD occurs with other mental health or addiction problems?

It is very common for someone with borderline personality disorder to have other mental health or substance use or gambling problems that can complicate the diagnosis and treatment of their BPD.

WHAT TYPES OF ADDICTION SERVICES ARE AVAILABLE?

Many people with BPD also have a substance use problem that may require specialized substance abuse treatment either on a community outpatient or residential basis. Community-based outpatient or day programs are effective for most people with a substance use problem, though a person with few resources and supports may require the more intensive treatment and support provided in a residential program. In Ontario, specific admission criteria and standardized assessment tools have been developed to guide individualized treatment planning and referral to the most appropriate treatment program.

As well as assessment and referral, the continuum of specialized treatment resources includes withdrawal management services, community treatment (outpatient), day treatment, residential treatment, supportive residential treatment and continuing care. Some specialized programming based on gender, age, language or culture is also available across the province. You can get information on substance abuse services available in your community from your local addiction assessment and referral service or the

Drug and Alcohol Registry of Treatment (DART). Specialized treatment definitions can be found on the DART website. Contact information for DART is given in Resources on p. 43.

In Ontario, treatment services for people with gambling problems are affiliated with substance abuse treatment services and available in many communities across Ontario. Information on gambling treatment is available through the Ontario Problem Gambling Helpline (see p. 43).

WHAT TYPES OF CONCURRENT DISORDER SERVICES ARE AVAILABLE?

Until recently, people with concurrent mental health and substance use disorders fell between the cracks because substance abuse and mental health services operated in isolation from each other. Staff members were often unwilling or felt unprepared to help someone with a concurrent disorder.

However, many services now recognize the importance of providing integrated treatment for both problems, particularly for people with severe mental health and substance use problems. Integrated treatment is a way of making sure that treatment is smooth, co-ordinated and complete. It also helps to ensure that the client understands the treatment plan. The client receives help not only with the concurrent disorders but also in other life areas, such as housing and employment. In integrated treatment, one person, such as a case manager or therapist, is responsible for overseeing the client's treatment, which is provided by a team of professionals. The team may include psychiatrists, social workers, psychiatric nurses, psychologists, vocational and occupational therapists, peer support workers and addiction therapists. This treatment may take place in a single setting, such as a residential facility, or through a mixture of different resources such as family doctors, hospital outpatient clinics and community outreach teams.

Integrated treatment is not always offered, but it is important that the primary therapist or treatment team co-ordinate their treatment with other services being used by your affected family member. More information about treatment for concurrent disorders can be found in *A Family Guide to Concurrent Disorders* listed in Publications on p. 44 at the end of this booklet.

Specialized psychosocial treatments for BPD

It's still "work" to use most of the skills I learned. I've seen some small changes in my interpersonal relationships and in my ability to manage my emotions more effectively.

— *a client*

There are a number of approaches for treatment of BPD. Two major approaches are cognitive behavioural therapy (CBT), which focuses on the present and on changing negative thoughts and behaviours, and psychodynamic therapy, which focuses on early relationships and inner conflicts. Treatment may be offered either individually or in a group. Family treatment is another mode of treatment that engages the whole family and works on relationships and interactions between family members.

There tends to be a high drop-out rate from treatment for borderline personality disorder, and a key to successful treatment is a good match between the therapist and client. Therapy might focus on learning to understand and manage emotions, harmful behaviours and thoughts of suicide. Medication may be used to make concentrating on learning self-management skills easier. Specialized treatments, now being developed and evaluated for BPD, use either a cognitive behavioural or psychodynamic framework. They have been developed and evaluated to be delivered by trained therapists in a specific way outlined in a manual. Some of these treatments have been more extensively evaluated than others. Clincians may use a variety of treatment approaches depending on the goals of the client and the skills base of the clinician. These may include:

- dialectical behaviour therapy
- cognitive behavioural therapy
- schema therapy
- system training for emotional predictability and problem solving
- transference-focused psychotherapy
- mentalization-based therapy.

Definitions of each of these therapies are included in the Glossary, p. 52.

Medication for BPD

Medication has a role in the treatment of many serious mental health problems. Though there is no specific medication for BPD, medication may be prescribed to reduce the impact of specific symptoms of the disorder. For example, medication may be prescribed to reduce depression or psychotic-like symptoms such as paranoia.

Medication can also be helpful to the person with BPD by providing a period of time when their symptoms are reduced. This allows them to focus on learning new skills to manage their behaviours with the goal of discontinuing medication when they are able to self-manage.

Though medication can reduce the severity of symptoms, medication does not cure BPD and medication is not appropriate for everyone with this diagnosis. The medications can have side-effects, and people may experience many, some or almost none of them. Side-effects can usually be addressed by changing the medication dosage or switching to another medication. Because of the number of different symptoms of BPD, there is also a risk that a person may be prescribed too many medications at the same time. Taking a number of different medications together can increase the risk of medication-related problems when:

- two or more medications, including prescribed, over-the-counter and herbal or other alternative medications, interact with each other to produce unwanted or unexpected effects, such as a greater or lesser effect than intended
- an individual has difficulty managing his or her medications (forgetting to take a medication or inadvertently taking extra doses of the medication)
- alcohol is taken at the same time as medication, which can make some medications less effective, or when it is combined with medications such as a benzodiazepine, which produces a greater than intended effect.

Most mental health medications are used to help restore chemical balance in the brain. They can help reduce the frequency and severity of symptoms. Medications are divided into four main groups based on the problems that they were developed to treat:

- antidepressants
- mood stabilizers
- anti-anxiety drugs
- antipsychotics.

Medications have a generic (or chemical) name and a brand (or trade) name that is specific to the company that makes the medication. For example, the generic drug lorazepam is sold under the brand name Ativan. The brand name may change depending on the country in which the medication is marketed.

ANTIDEPRESSANTS

Antidepressants are used to treat depression, as well as a number of other problems such as anxiety, chronic pain and bulimia. They work by increasing communication between nerve cells in the brain. A class of antidepressants called ssris (selective serotonin reuptake inhibitors) is most often prescribed for bpd. Some of the more common examples of ssri medications are paroxetine (Paxil), fluoxetine (Prozac), sertraline (Zoloft), citalopram (Celexa) and escitalopram (Cipralex).

MOOD STABILIZERS

Mood stabilizers are used to treat mood disorders, the most common of which is bipolar disorder (manic-depression). Mood stabilizers do not stabilize mood in bpd, but can help with outbursts of anger. Common examples are divalproex (Epival), carbamazepine (Tegretol), lamotrigine (Lamictal) and topiramate (Topamax).

ANTI-ANXIETY MEDICATIONS/SEDATIVES

The main group of medications in this class are benzodiazepines, commonly used to treat sleep or anxiety problems or as a muscle relaxant. Examples are lorazepam (Ativan), clonazepam (Rivotril) and diazepam (Valium). They are effective for short-term treatment of sleep or anxiety problems, but can be addictive when used over the longer term.

ANTIPSYCHOTICS

These medications are used to treat schizophrenia and other psychotic disorders. The first generation of antipsychotic medications is called typical antipsychotics. Some examples include haloperidol (Haldol), perphenazine (Trilafon), loxapine (Loxapac or Loxitane) and chlorpromazine (Largactil). Atypical antipsychotics are a second generation of antipsychotic drugs that are categorized together because they work differently from typical antipsychotic drugs, by working primarily on the receptors of the neurotransmitters serotonin and dopamine. Common examples of atypical antipsychotics are olanzapine (Zyprexa), risperidone (Risperdal) and quetiapine (Seroquel). These second generation antipsychotics also have some mood stabilizing properties and are being used this way as well.

Family members can play an important role in supporting their affected family member to:

- manage their medication by following prescribing instructions, and consult their physician or pharmacist if they have any concerns
- determine whether their medication is helpful in reducing unpleasant symptoms
- discuss their medication with their prescribing physician, its effects and side-effects and any difficulties they may be experiencing.

More information about different types of psychiatric medications can be found in *A Family Guide to Concurrent Disorders*, listed on p. 44 at the end of this booklet.

Recovery from BPD

Despite its often devastating effects on the affected person and his or her family, treatment outcome research has found that for many people, treatment does work. Many people with BPD do learn to cope with their symptoms and do things differently, particularly as they reach middle age. Because of the serious and complex nature of their symptoms, people affected by BPD often require long-term treatment, often over several years.

Treatment accelerates the natural process of recovery. Studies have followed people affected by BPD for extended periods of time and found that most improve with time. About 75 per cent will regain close to normal functioning by age 35 to 40 and 90 per cent will recover by age 50 (Paris, 2005).

It may take a longer time for a person with BPD to have a remission of their symptoms compared to people with other mental health problems, but when symptoms do decline, remission seems stable with few relapses compared to other serious mental health problems.

However, studies have also found that some BPD symptoms endure longer than others in some people. Some of the more harmful behaviours such as self-harm and suicidal behaviour decline while other symptoms such as feelings of abandonment and difficulty being alone may last longer.

Hope and recovery are important to both the person with BPD and his or her family members. These issues are discussed in more detail on p. 39.

4. Supporting the family member who has BPD

How can I support a person with BPD in seeking treatment?

Taking the steps to get help for a mental health problem can often seem overwhelming and frightening, even more so if the person has had distressing experiences in earlier contacts with the mental health treatment system. This is particularly true for people with BPD because of the complexity of their problems and the perception that they are "treatment resistant." As well, the person with BPD may not be able to see the value of treatment, particularly if prior treatment has not worked for them, and they may respond angrily or defensively to suggestions that they go for help.

Sometimes even asking for help can be difficult for someone whose culture does not encourage counselling or outside help. They may have difficulty finding the service they need because the counselling is not available or when it is, it is not in their language. You could contact your local cultural group to find out about culturally specific services or request an interpreter to work with the available treatment services.

If a person also has a substance use problem or some other problem that is the responsibility of "another system," he or she may have been turned away and told to go elsewhere. Unfortunately in some communities, the mental health and substance abuse treatment systems are not well co-ordinated, but progress is being made in many communities to better integrate them.

In the past, it was felt that "confronting" a family member about his or her problems would induce the person to accept treatment. In fact it often had the opposite effect. We cannot make someone go for treatment if they do not want to, however, there are some steps you can take to support your affected family member if and when they are ready to consider treatment:

- Learn about borderline personality disorder. It is important to understand that your affected family member has a health problem as much as anyone with a physical health problem, and that the behaviours you are observing are the symptoms of this health problem. It is also helpful to understand that BPD is a result of the interaction between genetic, biological and environmental vulnerabilities, rather than behaviours that the person has developed as a result of their own actions or intentions. Useful print materials and websites are listed at the end of this booklet.
- Find out about treatment resources in your community. Talking to your family doctor can be a good place to start to find out what kind of assistance your family member needs and what is available. You can also contact the Mental Health Service Information Ontario line (see p. 43) or your local branch of the Canadian Mental Health Association (see p. 47) if you have one. Other places to contact for help include psychiatric services at your local hospital, community mental health clinics, health and social service agencies serving specific cultural or language groups, your spiritual leader or faith-based counselling services, or a counsellor with your workplace Employee Assistance Program.
- Ask questions like these to determine the best match to the needs of your affected family member:
  1. Where is the facility located?
  2. Is it community- or hospital-based?

3. Is the program outpatient, day or residential?
4. What are the admission criteria and how does your family member get referred to the facility?
5. What type and length of program(s) is offered? Is it a specialized treatment program for BPD?
6. What languages are services offered in? Are translation services available?
7. What levels of professional staff are employed by the facility?
8. Is there an aftercare or continuing care program?
9. What level of involvement is available to family members? Is there a program for family members?
10. If your affected family member is female, is a female therapist available for individual counselling?
11. If your affected family member is female and if treatment is offered in groups, are they (co-)facilitated by a female therapist?
12. If the program is residential, are female-only areas such as sleeping areas provided?
13. If your affected family member has dependent children, is there any child care and/or programming available for children?
14. Is there a fee?

- Assist your family member to make an appointment.
- Offer to accompany her or him to the appointment if she or he would like your support.
- Obtain support for yourself either by attending a professionally run treatment/support program for family members or by attending a mutual-aid group. Education and support from others can help you in your relationship with your affected family member and may encourage him or her to seek help.
- Take care of yourself and encourage other family members to do the same.

INVOLUNTARY HOSPITAL ADMISSION

Family members often find it difficult to understand why their affected family member cannot always be involuntarily admitted to hospital for treatment so he or she can get the help needed. However, in Ontario and most other Canadian jurisdictions, a person can only be certified as an involuntary patient if a physician believes that he or she is likely to harm himself or herself (self-harming or suicidal) or someone else (violent) or suffer serious physical impairment (not eating, drinking, or taking required medications) due to a mental disorder. Under the Ontario *Mental Health Act* (MHA), a person can be brought into hospital under the following three conditions:

- When a person is acting in a disorderly manner, the police are allowed to bring the person to be examined by a physician if they believe the person is a danger to himself or herself or others or the person cannot care for himself or herself.
- In situations where there is no immediate danger, anyone can bring evidence to a Justice of the Peace (JP) that the person is a danger to himself or herself or others or cannot care for himself or herself and the Justice of the Peace can order that the person be examined by a physician. The JP is required to fill out a Form 2 that authorizes the police to take the person to a physician.
- If a physician has assessed a person within the last seven days and feels that a person may be a danger to himself or herself or to others or cannot care for himself or herself, the physician can order that the person be examined by a psychiatrist. The physician is required to fill out a Form 1 that authorizes the police to take the person for an examination.

Once the person is brought to a psychiatric facility, a physician may detain the person for up to 72 hours for psychiatric assessment, but no treatment is permitted without patient consent. After that time, a person must either be released or admitted as a voluntary or involuntary patient, as indicated in the *Mental Health Act*.

Recent changes to the MHA and the *Health Care Consent Act, 1996* (HCCA) allow family members of those with a serious mental illness and health care professionals to act at an earlier stage of a person's mental illness with revised committal criteria. These revised commital criteria allow them to implement procedures for treatment, care and supervision in the community through community treatment order (CTO) provisions. CTOs are designed to provide treatment in the community for individuals who may otherwise meet criteria for ongoing hospitalization. Specifically, a CTO candidate is someone who is likely to harm himself or herself or others or who is likely to suffer substantial mental or physical deterioration or physical impairment as a consequence of mental disorder, unless she or he receives continuing treatment/care or supervision in the community. Certain other criteria must also be met before the CTO is signed by the physician. Further information on CTOs can be found at www.health.gov.on.ca/english/public/pub/mental/faq.html.

WHAT TO DO IN A CRISIS

A Family Guide to Concurrent Disorders distinguishes between a crisis and an emergency. A crisis develops when "people feel they cannot control their feelings or behaviour and have trouble coping with the demands of day to day life." Potentially this can develop into outbursts of anger or violence or self-injuring behaviours. A crisis may develop slowly over a number of days or erupt suddenly. A particularly high-risk time for a crisis is when a person with BPD fears abandonment or loss of support. Such times may occur when a family member or a therapist is away for a period of time or when the person becomes fearful that the good progress they are making may lead to pressure to become more independent with consequent loss of support (Gunderson & Berkowitz).

Strategies for managing a crisis in the short term include:
- Stay calm and supportive of your family member. Do not get into a shouting match however difficult their behaviour, and

even if you are hurt by what they are saying.

- Acknowledge what your affected family member may be feeling or saying, let him or her know you have heard them and are trying to understand what they may be feeling.
- Don't be afraid to ask about suicidal intentions. Suicidal behaviours can be an attempt to relieve emotional pain or communicate distress.
- Act on the agreed upon crisis plan if one is already in place.
- Support your affected family member in making telephone contact with their doctor, therapist or treatment program or offer to drive them to where they need to go (e.g., therapist, hospital).
- If your family member has broken any agreements you have with them regarding their behaviour, wait until the crisis is over to discuss it.

You should also make a long-term plan for managing a crisis:

- Discuss with your affected family member and his or her doctor or therapist the steps to take if a crisis should occur.
- Make sure that your affected family member is involved in all decisions regarding the crisis plan and that his or her wishes are respected.
- Using the Family Crisis Information Sheet on p. 57, create a crisis plan with your family member and others in the family as appropriate.
- The crisis plan can include a section on who does what, for example, who should accompany your family member to the hospital, and who should communicate with the treatment team.
- Include important information as part of your crisis plan, for example, telephone numbers for your family member's family doctor, therapist and local hospital, and a list of the medications he or she is taking.
- Keep the crisis plan in a prominent place.
- You may wish to include information from the crisis plan on a

"crisis card" small enough for your affected family member to carry with her or him. The crisis card could also contain personal contact information, e.g., family member phone numbers, as well as a list of medications that he or she is taking and strategies to help them self-calm.

· Find out about crisis services in your community. If your family member is already known to the mental health system, you should ask whom you or your affected family member should contact if his or her behaviour deteriorates so this can be built into the crisis plan. Some communities have mobile crisis teams based at a local hospital psychiatric department who will come and assess the situation.

For more information on how to handle a crisis, see *A Family Guide to Concurrent Disorders,* listed on p. 44.

WHAT TO DO IN AN EMERGENCY

Sometimes a crisis can escalate into an emergency. Emergencies could be situations in which there are threats of suicide, threats of physical violence, reduced judgment and decision-making or substance use that concerns you.

In some circumstances, your family member will voluntarily agree to talk to his or her doctor or therapist or to go to the hospital emergency department. In other situations, you may need to call 911. This can be a difficult step to take. Inevitably the arrival of the police or other emergency services will arouse the curiosity of neighbours. Both you and your affected family member may wish to keep his or her mental health problem as a private matter, but safety is a priority, particularly when it involves potential harm or suicidal intentions. If you perceive any danger to yourself or anyone else, do not hesitate to leave and call 911 from somewhere else. When you call 911, tell the operator that your family member needs emergency medical assistance, give the operator your family member's diagnosis and tell the operator that you need help transporting him or her to the hospital.

Depending on the kind of training your local police have had in handling mental health crisis situations, you may need to advocate on behalf of your family member. This may be particularly important if your family member is likely to react negatively to the presence of uniformed police. It is useful to write down the names, badge numbers and response times of the officers who respond to the call in case you have any concerns about the way the problem was handled.

When the emergency involves suicidality

Threatening suicide is one type of emergency situation. Threatening suicide or expressing a wish to die should always be taken seriously.

Some warning signs of suicide include:
- feelings of despair, pessimism, hopelessness, desperation
- recent self-injury behaviours
- withdrawal from social circles
- sleep problems
- increased use of alcohol or other drugs or overeating
- winding up affairs or giving away prized possessions
- threatening suicide or expressing a desire to die
- talking about "when I am gone"
- talking about voices that tell him or her to do something dangerous
- having a plan and the means to carry it out.

SHARING TREATMENT INFORMATION WITH FAMILY MEMBERS

Generally speaking, sharing medical or treatment information about a person with others, either family members or outside health care providers or agencies, requires expressed consent. Consent in these situations would usually be written consent.

Family members can play a key role in supporting change and developing newly acquired skills. However, some health care professionals are reluctant to involve or talk to family members, particularly if they perceive the family as "causing the problem." If your family member is still living at home and/or you are supporting them financially, you may feel you should have some moral right to be involved in their treatment. However, if your family member is capable of making treatment decisions, a health care professional will not be at liberty to share information without your affected family member's consent. This is achieved by having your family member sign a form in the doctor's office.

Some treatment programs offer family programming. This may involve family therapy sessions with the person affected by BPD and his or her family members. More commonly, family-specific education/support groups provide information about the disorder, ways for family members to support the person with BPD and strategies for family members' self care.

CONSENT TO TREATMENT

In Ontario, individuals have the right to consent to or refuse treatment, provided they are capable of doing so. Being capable means that the person is able to understand the information needed to make this decision and is also able to appreciate the reasonably foreseeable consequences of their consent to or refusal of treatment. There is no age requirement on consenting to treatment; if a person is capable, she or he gets to make her or his own treatment decisions, regardless of age.

Consent to treatment must be "informed" (which means that the person has been given all the requisite information and all questions related to the treatment have been answered), must be given voluntarily and must not be obtained through misrepresentation or fraud. In situations where a person is not capable to give informed consent, then a substitute decision-maker would be consulted for treatment consent. The HCCA (Health Care Consent Act) sets up a hierarchy of individuals who may provide substitute consent.

HOW TO DEAL EFFECTIVELY WITH THE LEGAL SYSTEM IF A FAMILY MEMBER HAS A LEGAL PROBLEM

Ontario has court support and diversion programs in many communities. The role of these programs is to provide advocacy and support for people with mental health problems and their family members when they are involved with courts, police or other legal situations. Diversion programs are intended to divert people with a mental health problem who have committed minor offences from the criminal justice system into treatment and community support. The Mental Health Service Information Ontario line has a listing of advocacy and support programs, many of them sponsored by the Canadian Mental Health Association. This information line is listed under Resources on p. 43 at the end of this booklet.

The legal system can be a potentially frightening experience for a newcomer to Canada, particularly if they are not comfortable communicating in either English or French. Possible resources for advice and support might include an ethno-specific agency, a legal aid clinic experienced in serving newcomers to Canada, faith community leaders and cultural interpreter programs.

Your family member may also be referred for an assessment and possible treatment at a forensic facility if she or he has been found either unfit to stand trial or not criminally responsible for an offence by reason of mental disorder. Information about the forensic mental health system in Ontario can be found in *The Forensic Mental Health System in Ontario: An Information Guide* listed under Publications on p. 44 at the end of this booklet.

How can I support my family member during treatment?

Treatment for BPD is a long-term endeavour, often requiring a commitment of a number of years. Progress is not always straight forward and there will be diversions along the way with relapse back to old behaviours in times of stress or crisis. Some guidelines suggested for helping your affected family member include:

- Support your affected family member in the treatment program by encouraging him or her to attend treatment, take the medication as prescribed and lead a healthy lifestyle by eating well, exercising, getting enough rest and remaining abstinent from substances if this is a problem area.
- Recognize that change can be stressful and difficult to achieve. Making progress in treatment, acquiring new skills, and becoming more independent can bring up fears that family members will start to withdraw protection and support and the person will be abandoned to manage on his or her own. These fears can lead to a relapse back to previous negative coping methods such as self-injury or a suicide attempt. It is important that family members support progress with words and encouragement that let their affected family member know they understand how difficult change is.
- Support your family member to set realistic goals, and to work on them one at a time, one step at a time. Though you don't want to discourage your family member, it is very important to keep in mind the fine balance between a desire for independence and fears of abandonment. For example, a realistic goal might be enrolling in one university course for a semester rather than signing up for full-time classes; finding employment that he or she can manage or moving into a group home rather than moving out of the family home directly into independent living.

- Maintain a cool and calm environment when dealing with conflict or a crisis. It is important to recognize that some of the symptoms of BPD, including intense and painful emotions, inability to deal with even small separations from significant people, and black and white (all good, all bad) thinking about people or situations can easily lead to family conflict or a crisis. Take time to listen, or make a time later if you are unable to deal with it at that moment. The important thing is for your family member with BPD to be heard and validated.

- Remain optimistic, though change may be slow. The periods of time when symptoms are absent or much reduced will increase as your family member and you learn new skills for dealing with relapses.

- Most important, don't feel the responsibility is all yours to solve problems and be responsible. It is important to allow your affected family member to be in charge, try new behaviours and be responsible for negative behaviours.

- If you are concerned, contact your family doctor or your family member's treatment provider, or in emergency situations call 911.

5. Self-care

Caring for yourself when a family member has BPD

I am learning to refocus on my own needs and taking better care of myself.

— *a client's parent*

Borderline personality disorder can be as devastating for partners, parents, children and others close to a person with BPD, as it is for the person himself or herself. As a family member, you may have had many years of trying to cope with the intense anger, suicide attempts, self-injury or other impulsive behaviours that are part of BPD. As a result, you may feel weighed down by the burden of your family member's illness. Depression, anxiety, grief and isolation are some feelings you may have experienced.

Even though care and support of your affected family member may seem to be all you can manage, making time to care for your own needs is a priority. Self-care can reduce stress and give you more energy and patience to support a family member with BPD. Self-care can involve seeking support from a community agency that provides family counselling services, joining a mutual-aid group, signing up for an exercise class, or reconnecting with family and friends.

Some services for people with BPD offer facilitated family programs on either an individual family basis or as part of a support group for family members. These programs provide information about the issues related to BPD, new communication and coping skills and most important, support from others in the same situation. Groups may be facilitated by a health care professional or by a trained family member. Your community may also have self-help groups for family members. Additionally, some family members may also benefit from individual counselling sessions as well as the family group support.

ACKNOWLEDGING AND ADDRESSING GRIEF

Grief is a normal response to loss, whether the loss is the death of a child or loss of a child because of a serious and chronic illness. Grieving may be accompanied by feelings of anxiety about how one will cope, guilt about whether the family has in some way contributed to the onset of BPD, anger about what has happened and a feeling of helplessness to change things.

Both the individual with BPD and his or her family may grieve the perceived losses that result from a serious mental illness such as lost expectations and potential. Some feelings of loss may include loss of their child's role in the family and society, academic and professional expectations and healthy relationships for their child.

Parents also experience internal losses such as loss of self-esteem and feelings of competence as a parent, loss of dreams for a child, loss of hope and security, loss of faith, loss of a normal family life. Grief may not be recognized and validated by others such as other family members, friends, or health professionals, but it is important that family members find ways of working through their grief so they can move forward to accept their child's illness and its implications for the future (MacGregor, 1994).

LIMIT-SETTING

Families will often go to great lengths to protect their affected family member from the consequences of her or his behaviour. However, if a person does not experience the consequences of his or her problem behaviour, it is likely to persist. At the same time, family members can become angry that they are continually picking up the pieces. Experiencing the consequences of one's behaviour can sometimes be the first step toward change.

Setting limits on problem behaviour can reduce family conflict and provide a more secure and predictable environment for everyone in the family. There are three important steps identified by Gunderson and Berkowitz when solving a family member's problems:
- involve the family member in identifying what needs to be done
- ask whether the person can "do" what's needed in the solution
- ask whether they want you to help them "do" what's needed.

Limit-setting involves an understanding of how a problem behaviour develops and is maintained, and how desired behaviours can be increased and undesirable behaviours decreased. For example, you may want to increase the frequency of your affected family member talking to you without getting angry. Verbal praise, listening to what they are saying or some other positive reinforcing response can increase the frequency of this behaviour.

Negative reinforcement such as not listening or leaving the room when your family member is angry or shouting can decrease the frequency of this behaviour.

Some undesirable behaviours are maintained because they are inadvertently positively reinforced. Some people label this "enabling" because the person is enabled to continue their problem behaviour while someone else deals with the consequences or picks up the pieces. An example might be providing excuses to your family member's therapist when they miss an appointment, rather than having the person phone himself or herself and explain.

STRESS MANAGEMENT

Having a family member with BPD can seem overwhelming, especially if that family member is living at home and requires help in managing their activities of daily living and some aspects of their treatment regimen. People experience stress in different ways. We may experience physical symptoms such as headaches, difficulty sleeping, stomach upsets, weight gain or loss. We may experience emotional symptoms such as moodiness, restlessness, feeling overwhelmed or depressed. We may experience cognitive symptoms such as memory problems, racing thoughts, chronic worrying or fearfulness. We may experience behavioural symptoms such as eating less or eating more, using substances to relax, over-reacting to situations or isolating ourselves socially.

People pay a high price in terms of their emotional and physical health when they live with chronic stress, so it is important to look at ways to reduce stress. There are many resources, both print materials and on the web, that provide advice on strategies for stress reduction. These include improving one's diet, building in regular exercise, learning relaxation exercises, building in enjoyable activities (e.g., having a massage, engaging in a hobby), changing the stressful situation (for example, setting limits for your family member's behaviour), obtaining support from others (for example, involving other family members or friends), joining a support group, and drawing on sources of spiritual support.

In developing a self-care plan to reduce your level of stress, it is important to keep your plan realistic and doable. Small changes will make you feel better and have more chance of success than big changes that run the risk of being unsuccessful and thereby further contributing to your stress. Your plan should also be concrete and identify what needs to happen for the plan to be successful. For example, you decide to go to an exercise class once a week; in order for this to be successful you may need to have another family member cook a meal or enlist a friend to go with you for mutual support.

Helping children understand and cope with BPD

Children can be affected when a family member has BPD. To protect their children, parents may say nothing. They may try to continue with family routines as if nothing were wrong. This strategy may work in the short term but not in the long term. Children can feel confused and worried about their family member's behaviour when they are not given the opportunity to talk about it. Children are sensitive and intuitive. They quickly notice when someone in the family has changed, particularly a parent. If the family doesn't talk about the problem, children will draw their own, often wrong, conclusions.

Young children, especially those in preschool or early grades, often see the world as revolving around themselves. If something happens, they think they caused it. For example, a child may accidentally break something valuable. The next morning, the parent may seem very depressed. The child may then think that breaking the object caused the parent's depression.

Older children, particularly if they have a sibling with BPD, may worry about developing mental health problems, substance use problems or both. They may worry about the stress and strain that their parents are enduring, and may take on the burden of trying to make up for what their parents have lost in their other child.

At the same time, brothers or sisters sometimes resent the time that parents spend with their sibling. They may become angry to the point of acting out or distancing themselves from family or friends. Siblings may also experience anger, hostility or verbal or physical aggression from their brother or sister. These behaviours can evoke shock, dismay, fear and a sense of abandonment and rejection. Sometimes, children may feel like they have lost their best friend. They may feel guilty that they have a better life than their brother or sister.

HOW MUCH SHOULD I TELL THE CHILDREN?

Children need to have things explained. Give them as much information as they can understand, and that is appropriate to their age.

It is helpful to tell children three main points:

The family member has a problem called borderline personality disorder. The family member behaves this way because he or she is sick. The illness may have symptoms that can cause the person's mood or behaviour to change in unpredictable ways.

The child did not cause the problems. Children need reassurance that they did not make the parent or family member sad, angry or unhappy. They need to be told that their behaviour did not cause the person's emotions or behaviour. Children think in concrete terms. If a parent or family member is sad or angry, children can easily feel they did something to cause this, and then feel guilty.

It is not the child's responsibility to make the affected person well. Children need to know that the adults in the family, and other people, such as doctors, are working to help the person. It is the adults' job to look after the person with the problem.

Children need the well parent(s) and other trusted adults to shield them from the effects of the person's symptoms. It is hard for children to see their parents distressed or emotional. Talking with someone who understands the situation can help sort out the child's feelings (Skinner et. al., 2004; O'Grady & Skinner, 2007).

6. Recovery and hope

I am learning to deal with loss and grief and accept my daughter
for who she is. I am not expecting a perfect ending but I do
have more hope for the future and I know I am not alone.
— a family client

Research has shown that people can recover from BPD and that
their recovery is often long-lasting.

Everyone's path to recovery is different, whether you are the individual with BPD or a family member or friend. Recovery involves
the development of new meaning and purpose in life as people
grow beyond the impact of BPD. We think O'Grady and Skinner
(2007) say it best: "Recovery has also been described as a process
by which people recover their self-esteem, dreams, self-worth,
empowerment, pride, dignity and meaning."

Both the individual with BPD and their family members will go
through this process of recovery. As a family member, you can
instill hope that changes can be achieved by providing support to
your loved one as you all go through the long journey of recovery.

It is important to understand though that recovery is not a straight path.
There will be deviations along the way that can involve relapse into old
behaviours, and the person may or may not return to their previous
level of functioning. On the path to recovery, your family member
may need medication or further contact with the treatment system.

For people to achieve and maintain recovery from BPD, they need to:

- be treated as unique and important
- be treated as a human being with goals and dreams
- have the freedom to make choices and decisions about their lives
- be treated with dignity and respect
- accept that their unique journey through life has taken a different path
- recognize that recovery is the potential to become free of symptoms by following an individualized treatment plan
- acknowledge that relapse is a common and expected part of recovery, but does not mean they have "failed" or that previous gains are lost, rather, it is a chance to learn and move forward again
- have hope about their future
- engage in meaningful relationships with others who care and do not stigmatize
- have a routine and structure to their day marked by meaningful activities that may or may not include work (paid or volunteer)
- receive a reliable and steady source of income
- live in stable, clean and comfortable housing, whether it is an independent living situation or supportive housing
- accept that recovery may require a structured community day treatment program or other links to professional mental health and addiction systems of care
- recognize that pets may be important
- recognize that spirituality or religious beliefs and practices may be important.

More information on recovery is available in *A Family Guide to Concurrent Disorders,* listed on p. 44.

7. Conclusion

Borderline personality disorder is one of the most common and most misunderstood of the serious mental health disorders. People living with BPD are often stigmatized and avoided by treatment providers. New treatments are emerging and with the right treatment, people with BPD can and do recover. Unlike other serious mental health problems, recovery from BPD is usually stable. Families play a crucial role in supporting their affected family member's recovery, but families also need support and nurturing to recover from the impact of their family member's illness. We hope that the information in this guide is helpful to you, and to others who may have someone with BPD in their lives.

REFERENCES

DBTSF [Dialectical Behaviour Therapy San Francisco]. (2006). Helping Someone with BPD. Available: www.dbtsf.com/helping-someone.htm. Accessed January 7, 2009.

Grant, B.F., Chou, S.P., Goldstein, R.B., Huang, B. et al. (2008). Prevalence, correlates, disability, and comorbidity of DSM-IV borderline personality disorder: results from the Wave 2 National Epidemiologic Survey on Alcohol and Related Conditions. *Journal of Clinical Psychiatry, 69*, 533–45.

Gunderson J.G. & Berkowitz, C. (n.d.). Family Guidelines: Multiple Family Group Program at McLean Hospital. The New England Personalty Disorder Association. Available: www.nepda.org/family_connections. Accessed January 7, 2009.

MacGregor, P. (1994). Grief: the Unrecognized Parental Response to Mental Illness in a Child. *Social Work, 19* (2), 160–166.

O'Grady, C.P. & Skinner, W.J.W. (2007). *A Family Guide to Concurrent Disorders* (pp. 185; 56). Toronto: Centre for Addiction and Mental Health.

Paris, J. (2005). Borderline personality disorder. *Canadian Medical Association Journal, 172* (12), 1579–1583.

Skinner, W.J.W.; O'Grady, C.P., Bartha, C. & Parker, C. (2004). *Concurrent Substance Use and Mental Health Disorders: An Information Guide* (pp. 35–38). Toronto: Centre for Addiction and Mental Health.

Williams, L. (1998). A classic case of Borderline Personality Disorder. *Psychiatric Services, 49* (29), 173–174. Available: www.psychservices.psychiatryon line.org/cgi/content/full/49/2/173?eaf. Accessed January 7, 2009.

RESOURCES

Information about treatment resources in Ontario

Connex*Ontario* is a bilingual information and referral service for the public and professionals in Ontario who want to access addiction and mental health treatment for themselves, family, friends or clients. Information and referral specialists offer education and guidance based on each caller's situation. Connex*Ontario* operates its own website and the following toll-free telephone numbers:

www.connexontario.ca

Drug and Alcohol Registry of Treatment (DART)
1 800 565-8603
www.dart.on.ca

Mental Health Service Information Ontario (MHSIO)
1 866 531-2600
www.mhsio.on.ca

Ontario Problem Gambling Helpline (OPGH)
1 888 230-3505
www.opgh.on.ca

CAMH Publications

The Centre for Addiction and Mental Health offers several print and web-based resources that may be of interest:

A Family Guide to Concurrent Disorders by Caroline P. O'Grady and W.J. Wayne Skinner was created based on materials developed for a support and education group for family members of those with concurrent mental health and substance use problems. It contains information and educational material, quotations from family members, resources and contact information, tip lists and activities. It addresses in greater detail many of the issues addressed here in *Borderline Personality Disorder: An information guide for families* www.camh.net/Care_Treatment/Resources_clients_families_friends/ Family_Guide_CD/.

Concurrent Substance Use and Mental Health Disorders: An Information Guide, 2004

www.camh.net/About_Addiction_Mental_Health/Concurrent_ Disorders/Concurrent_Disorders_Information_Guide/

The Forensic Mental Health System in Ontario: An Information Guide

www.camh.net/Care_Treatment/Resources_clients_families_friends/ Forensic_Mental_Health_Ontario/index.html

Looking for Mental Health Services: What You Need to Know

www.camh.net/About_Addiction_Mental_Health/Mental_Health_
Information/looking_menthealth_services.html

Challenges and Choices: Finding Mental Health Services in Ontario

www.camh.net/Care_Treatment/Resources_clients_families_friends
/Challenges_and_Choices/index.html

Other online publications

Medications, published by the U.S. National Institute of
   Mental Health

www.nimh.nih.gov/health/publications/medications/summary.shtml

Canada's Food Guide, published by Health Canada

Maintaining health through healthy eating is important for both
people with BPD and their families. *Eating Well with Canada's Food
Guide* provides information on how much and what types of food
are needed and the benefits of healthy eating.

www.hc-sc.gc.ca/fn-an/food-guide-aliment/order-commander/
index-eng.php

Physical Activity Guide, published by the Public Health Agency
   of Canada

Maintaining health through physical activity is important for both
people with BPD and their families. The *Physical Activity Guide*
provides information on the benefits of being active, how much
activity you should aim for and examples of different types of
physical activity.

www.phac-aspc.gc.ca/pau-uap/paguide/index.html

Stress, a pamphlet published by the Canadian Mental
   Health Association

www.marketingisland.com/CMHA/pages/product.asp?id=2672
(under the image of the pamphlet, select View English PDF or
View French PDF)

A BPD Brief: An Introduction to Borderline Personality Disorder
   by John G. Gunderson, M.D.

www.borderlinepersonalitydisorder.com (select the "Reading" tab,
then select "A BPD Brief")

Books about BPD

New Hope for People with Borderline Personality Disorder (2002) by
Neil R. Bockian and Nora Elizabeth Villagran. New York: Three
Rivers Press.

*Stop Walking on Eggshells: Taking Your Life Back When Someone
You Care About Has Borderline Personality Disorder* (1998) by
Paul T. Mason and Randi Kreger. Oakland, CA: New Harbinger
Publications, Inc.

*The Stop Walking on Eggshells Workbook: Practical Strategies for
Living With Someone Who Has Borderline Personality Disorder*
(2002) by Randi Kreger and James Paul Shirley. Oakland,
CA: New Harbinger Publications, Inc.

*Understanding and Treating Borderline Personality Disorder: A Guide
for Professionals and Families* (2005) edited by John G. Gunderson
and Perry D. Hoffman. American Psychiatric Publishing, Inc.

When Someone You Love has Borderline Personality Disorder: How to Repair the Relationship (2007) by Valerie Porr. Oakland, CA: New Harbinger Publications, Inc.

Internet Resources

CANADIAN WEBSITES

Centre for Addiction and Mental Health

www.camh.net

Canadian Mental Health Association, Ontario

www.ontario.cmha.ca

OTHER WEBSITES

Disclaimer: The websites listed below are for information only and are working sites as of November 2008. We have included information or a quote taken from each site to give you an idea of what their mission is. No endorsement by the Centre for Addiction and Mental Health (CAMH) should be inferred.

BPD Central
"Borderline Personality Disorder Information and Support."

www.bpdcentral.com/resources/basics/main.shtml

BPD411.org
"The information provided here has been tailored to the unique needs and experiences of people whose lives have been affected by someone who suffers from BPD or BPD traits. This site is not for those suffering from the disorder."

www.bpd411.org/

Behavioral Tech Research Inc.
"Behavioral Tech, LLC, founded by Dr. Marsha Linehan, trains mental health care providers and treatment teams who work with complex and severely disordered populations to use compassionate, scientifically valid treatments and to implement and evaluate these treatments in their practice setting."

www.behavioraltech.com

Borderline Personality Disorder Resource Center
"The Borderline Personality Disorder Resource Center (BPDRC) at New York-Presbyterian Hospital-Weill Cornell Medical College has been set up specifically to help those impacted by the disorder find the most current and accurate information on the nature of BPD, and on sources of available treatment."

www.bpdresourcecenter.org/

DBTSF [Dialectical Behavior Therapy San Francisco]: Helping Someone with BPD.
"This site is designed to provide information for people (or the loved ones of people) who need help with controlling emotions and self destructive behavior, as well as to let you know how I [Michael Baugh] work with individuals, couples and families in San Francisco and Daly City. These web pages contain information and links to other sites about Dialectical Behavior Therapy (DBT), Borderline Personality Disorder (BPD), and the therapeutic approaches I use with couples and families."

www.dbtsf.com/helping-someone.htm

Laura Paxton
This website is set up to sell Laura Paxton's book and workbook *Bordeline and Beyond.*

www.laurapaxton.com/

Marsha M. Linehan
This site has the works, books, papers, biographies and links of Marsha M Linehan.

http://faculty.washington.edu/linehan/

National Alliance on Mental Illness [NAMI]
"NAMI is the National Alliance on Mental Illness, the nation's [U.S.A.] largest grassroots organization for people with mental illness and their families. Founded in 1979, NAMI has affiliates in every state and in more than 1,100 local communities across the country."

www.nami.org/

National Education Alliance for Borderline Personality Disorder
"Advancing the BPD Agenda: The mission of the National Education Alliance for Borderline Personality Disorder (NEABPD) is to raise public awareness, provide education, promote research on borderline personality disorders, and enhance the quality of life of those affected by this serious mental illness."

www.borderlinepersonalitydisorder.com/

National Institute of Mental Health [NIMH]
"NIMH envisions a world in which mental illnesses are prevented and cured. The mission of NIMH is to transform the understanding and treatment of mental illnesses through basic and clinical research, paving the way for prevention, recovery and cure."

www.nimh.nih.gov/health/publications/borderline-personality-disorder.shtml

Parents Needing Understanding, Tenderness and Support (NUTS)
"NUTS means parents Needing Understanding, Tenderness and Support to help their child with Borderline Personality Disorder. For parents who are suffering over broken dreams and lives of turmoil; welcome to a place of refuge where beacons of light

will guide you to a safe harbor filled with understanding, comfort, and hope."

www.parent2parentbpd.org/?page_id=5

Personality Disorders Institute

"The Personality Disorders Institute offers the following information to the general public to enhance awareness of the particulary challenging psychiatric conditions known as borderline disorders or borderline personalities. Many patients struggle not only with symptoms such as depression, anxieties, obsessions or phobias for which help is typically sought, but also with control of emotion and agression, understanding of self, and tolerance of the treatment process. The discussion leads you through diagnosis, focusing on history and symptoms, and possible causes, treatments and outcomes. Contact and emergency information follows."

www.borderlinedisorders.com/public.htm

Treatment and Research Advancements, National Association for Personality Disorder (TARA APD)

"Founded in November of 1994 by Valerie Porr, MA, in response to the realization that patients with personality disorders are stigmatized by the mental health community, as a group are underdiagnosed, have little or no information available on etiology, nosology and treatment, and have little or no effective treatment available to them. Families, trying to cope with difficult behavior without necessary skills, understanding, insight, support or guidance are devastated and hopeless. Improving treatment would be cost effective. TARA APD refers people nationwide to clinicians and treatment programs that use empirically based treatment modalities. We operate the only BPD hotline in the nation, we also send each caller an educational packet on BPD."

www.tara4bpd.org/dyn/index.php

Welcome to Oz Online Community for Family Members
"Having a family member with Borderline Personality Disorder can make you feel all alone, with no one to talk to who really understands. And real life support groups are nearly impossible to find. That's why Randi Kreger, author, advocate, and owner of BPDCentral.com, started the Welcome to Oz online family community in 1996. wto is a sacred place where you'll meet new friends who know just what you're facing because they've been there too. There, you'll experience understanding and comfort and learn tips and techniques that have worked for others. wto members are wonderfully supportive and can carry you through both good and bad times."

www.bpdcentral.com/support/email.shtml

GLOSSARY

Unless otherwise noted, all definitions originate in CAMH publications.

affect. The current, observable state of feeling or emotion, such as sadness, anger or elation. (Manitoba Schizophrenia Society; www.mss.mb.ca/defin.htm)

alienation. Refers to the "separation" of people from control over many material and social aspects of their lives.
(www.oup.com/uk/orc/bin/9780199253975/01student/glossary/glossary.htm)

cognition. The mental process of knowing, including aspects such as awareness, perception, reasoning and judgment. (www.geocities.com/seaskj/glossary.html)

cognitive behavioural therapy (CBT). Probably the most widely used treatment for all types of mental health problems. The focus of this approach is on helping individuals change unhelpful thoughts, feelings and behaviours. The focus is on the present and helping people see how negative thoughts can lead to bad feelings and problem behaviours and supporting them to make changes by replacing unhelpful thoughts with positive thoughts and healthy behaviours.

concurrent disorders. Refers to conditions in which people have both a mental health and substance use problem.

co-occurring disorders (COD). Another way of describing a situation where someone has one or more mental health disorders and one or more substance use disorders. It can also refer to any combination of disorders that a person is experiencing at the same time.

dialectical behaviour therapy (DBT). Based on the biosocial theory of borderline personality disorder that views BPD as the consequence of an emotionally vulnerable individual growing up in an environment that is invalidating or dysfunctional with the affected individual experiencing difficulties in the areas of emotions, relationships, cognition and sense of self. DBT was initially developed by Marsha Linehan, and uses approaches that focus on the here and now and are designed to overcome the lack of self-validation experienced by the person living with BPD and to help her or him acquire the skills to deal more adaptively with these difficulties.

dissociation. A change in one's perception or experience of oneself and/or the external world. A feeling of "spacing out" or daydreaming.

DSM-IV-TR. The *Diagnostic and Statistical Manual of Mental Disorders (DSM)* is used in North America to diagnose mental disorders. A text revision of the fourth and most recent edition, the *DSM-IV-TR*, organizes mental disorders into 16 major diagnostic classes (e.g., mood disorders and substance-related disorders). Within these diagnostic classes, disorders are further broken down (e.g., depressive disorders and bipolar disorders are included in the mood disorders class). For each disorder, the *DSM-IV* lists specific criteria for making a diagnosis.

epidemiology. The study of the occurrence of disease and other health-related conditions in specified populations. (*Concise Dictionary of Modern Medicine*)

ethnocultural. An adjective that refers to a group of people who share and identify with certain common traits, such as language, ancestry, homeland, history and cultural traditions. In this guide, ethnocultural communities are defined as those communities whose members have ethnic origins that are not French, British or Aboriginal. While these communities often include newcomers, it is important to remember they also include people whose roots in Canada go back more than one generation.

integrated treatment. Treatment for substance use and mental health problems are combined and ideally provided in the same treatment setting by the same clinicians and support workers, or the same team of clinicians and support workers. This ensures that a client receives a consistent explanation of substance use and mental health problems and a coherent treatment plan. The client gets co-ordinated and comprehensive treatment, as well as help in other life areas, such as housing and employment. Ongoing support in these life areas helps clients to maintain treatment successes, prevent relapses and meet their basic life needs.

Justice of the Peace. A judicial officer who has authority to do a variety of things in criminal matters, including issuing warrants and orders of examination under the Mental Health Act, and hearing bail applications and provincial offence trials.

mentalization-based therapy (MBT). A psychodynamic therapy that emphasizes individual recognition of the person's own mental states as well as those of others as a way of explaining behaviours.

neurosis. A mental illness in which insight is retained but there is a maladaptive way of behaving or thinking that causes suffering, for example, depression, anxiety, phobias or obsessions. (www.rohcg.on.ca/resources/glossary-e.cfm?strSearch=neurosis)

obsessive-compulsive disorder (OCD). Patients with this disorder have intrusive thoughts (obsessions) or the urge to perform irresistible repetitive acts (rituals). The performance of these acts/behaviours may reduce anxiety.

panic disorder. An anxiety disorder characterized by attacks of severe anxiety, terror or fear.

posttraumatic stress disorder (PTSD). A condition of re-experiencing the effects of a traumatic event long after the event is over.

predisposition. The state of being predisposed; a tendency, inclination, or susceptibility.

prevalence. Frequency of a disorder, used particularly in epidemiology to denote the total number of cases existing within a unit of population at a given time or over a specified period. (www.mentalhealth.com)

primary care. The first level of care, and usually the first point of contact, that people have with the health care system. It includes advice on health promotion and disease prevention, assessments of one's health, diagnosis and treatment of episodic and chronic conditions, and supportive and rehabilitative care. (Ministry of Health: Primary Health Care Strategy, 1999)

psychiatrist. A person with a medical degree and five years of psychiatric training. Because psychiatrists are medical doctors, they are licensed to prescribe medication and provide psychotherapy. Their services are covered by OHIP. As medical doctors, they are more likely to identify connections between psychiatric and physical health problems. Some clients report that psychiatrists tend to be more focused on medication than on talking therapy, perhaps because of their medical training. However, some psychiatrists put emphasis on psychotherapy in their practice.

psychoeducational. A process or aspect of a process that allows people to recognize and learn how to manage their psychiatric illness.

psychosis/psychotic. Refers to disturbances/describes a condition where disturbances cause someone's personality to break down. The person loses touch with reality; he or she may imagine hearing voices or seeing things or believe things that seem untrue.

recovery. A process, an outlook, a vision and a guiding principle. Recovery has also been described as a process by which people recover their self-esteem, dreams, self-worth, empowerment, pride, dignity and meaning. For professionals and families, recovery is about treating the whole person: identifying their strengths, instilling hope, helping them to function by helping them take responsibility for their lives.

registered psychologist. The College of Psychologists of Ontario regulates the profession of psychology in Ontario. Members of the College of Psychologists are regulated professionals and are the only persons authorized to practise psychology in the province. Psychologists and Psychological Associates are members of the College of Psychologists. (www.cpo.on.ca)

residential treatment. Intensive treatment, for which a person stays at a treatment facility 24 hours a day. These programs vary in length from a few weeks to several months.

schema therapy. Therapeutic approach based on cognitive behavioural or skills-based therapy, but also targets deeper aspects of emotions, personality and schemas that are ways in which an individual categorizes the world.

social phobia. A significant amount of anxiety and self-consciousness in everyday social situations. Affected people worry about being judged by others and embarrassed by their own actions. This anxiety can lead them to avoid potentially humiliating situations. Other symptoms such as blushing, sweating, trembling, problems talking or nausea can also occur. Women are twice as likely as men to develop social phobia, which typically begins in childhood or early adolescence.

stigma. Refers to the negative attitudes people have toward people with mental health problems, leading to prejudice and unfair and discriminatory behaviour.

substance use. Many people use alcohol, tobacco and even marijuana in moderate amounts and don't experience any problems. However, some people may start using larger amounts regularly, or using other substances to get intoxicated. These behaviours can lead to problems with a person's job, family and health. After repeated abuse, some people may become dependent on the substance.

System Training for Emotional Predictability and Problem Solving (STEPPS). A cognitive behavioural approach that teaches clients skills of emotional and behavioural regulation. This is reinforced by also teaching methods to family and friends that reinforce and support these new skills.

Transference-focused psychotherapy (TFP). Though this treatment is based on psychodynamic concepts, it also incorporates some behavioural elements, in particular setting up a treatment contract and framework with the client and addressing some of the behavioural symptoms of BPD.